D1441204

Gusenstein's Galaxies

~~JJ McNiece~~

H M' Ni

5/2020

Gusenstein's Galaxies

ISBN-13: 9781989305065

Six Gallery Press

Pittsburgh USA

For Karen

Contents

Part 1   **Gusenstein**

Part 2   **Nuclear**

Part 3   **Allegory of the Shell**

Part 1

Gusenstein

sil-ver-back: n. *Gorilla gorilla.* **1** dominant male mountain mammal with primate, hominidae tendencies—pec pounding, poacher punching patriarch who trains for snares tearing at bear traps. **2** stardust-sprinkled scar. **3** laboratory-made monster who seeks revenge on his creator. **4** convict behind a magic mirror. **5** learner of sign language. **6** parachute for caterpillars.

On a Soapbox

There is wisdom entrenched within us
Trusted teachers strangle and stab it

We choke on abuse
suffered then served across generations—
a syndicated rerun

We bleed and don't understand why
we are pulled to creators

In a dazed haste bandaging lacerations
we forget—
A soul remains stainless
steel

Only hearts and minds
    bear trauma and scars
        as we ride sublime
            clouds of stardust

Nightlight

Cicadas rooster dusk's dawn
Percussion ushers brass
            to bed with a timpani roll
Fireflies and eyes are symbiotic—
            a theater dims before a performance
Curtains of humidity part
The moon spotlights
            a protagonist's soliloquy
                  A pinhole peephole punctured
            into the façade of a world of light—
a kindled vestibule posing as a glare
Open wide or squinted?
The choice defines careers
Haloed spots and dots float
            if an actor even blinks
So let retinas melt
Let sweat pool
Let it drip into a surrealist stew
Slow cook the salty watered-down vision
Lift the lid—let the audience float
            above red velvet seats and waft
                  fish-hooked to a cartoon trope
Beguile fiction for a soup kitchen
Lunar limelight paves potholes
            in the primrose path
                  Outpace the vaudeville
            hook and stick a crooked neck
through the hole in the sky
Morpheus is serving eyeball soup
Sate your sockets
Take a bow
            to cock-a-doodle-doo

Balding

Gus, a quarter-ton silverback gorilla, sat with his back turned. Anchored to the corner of a solitary cage. When he caught preteen me staring at his balding purple scalp, he quickly whipped a long-lipped scowl. His nose looked like the mold of a clenched fist, and his eyes were pupiled tangerine marbles that glowed just like a person's.

I froze. He knew I had been staring at his baldness. In an instant he would pound his shaggy monster arms against the bars, gnash his teeth, roar and rip at his cage while I stood in a puddle of my own making.

But Gus forgave me. He returned to his solitude, and I timidly but politely nodded goodbye.

Twenty-three years later, Gus is in my mirror.

Gusenstein's Monster I

With a smear
        a star decays
        across a page

Black ink precipitates
    rainbows in a supernova

Painted streams pause and pixilate

I grab the beading strings
    to weave with them
    the whisper of the world—David's perfect chord
        double-helixed and stitched from the
            immaculate excrement

I knot two ends of a chromosome
    for a string game
Jacob's ladder peaks the pinnacle
    of Purgatory and I rifle Paradise
        for blueprints on riding lightning bolts
Angels laugh at Heaven's larcenist
  and the madness
   in his eyes
        A Seraphim picks "Chagrin"
        on a mandolin
But feral fevers
    near the presence of the Divine
        Cosmic Scientist's kiss of creation
    purging wit and senses with each bead of sweat
        splashing on the cloudy carpet

Gorilla Meets Owl

After Gregory Orr's The Caged Owl

I.

Poets are pen pals
incarcerated in cages.
Bars on the bottom
the top and all four walls
greased with defecation:
attempted escape routes.
A ring and a swollen finger will kiss
a rancid stick of butter.

A gloomy gorilla greets
the menagerie's Archimedes.
Confined for fratricide.
The owl whoos of animals, bones and snow.
Learning is the silverback's steroid.
He beats his breast.
Grips soiled steel and pries.
But calloused fingers slip
and he tumbles backward.

II.

I lie on a floor of tiled air, where I am
bitten by a scrap of paper.
Unfolded, a note with a snow globe's scene
living beneath the words.
I am absorbed into its storm.
My cage replaced by a boneyard
burying in a blizzard.
I make hand-shaped footprints.

Chimney smoke lures like hot pie.
Inside a log cabin, I find Merlin and his owl.
When he sees me, the wizard's skin melts.
A skeleton stands from his stool
and unlocks the birdcage. Archimedes flies

past me and through an open window. I look
down at the floor: a talon glints.
The room dissolves and I discover
I am again inside my cage.
I tear at the bars. Then I am
struck by a paper airplane.

Gusenstein's Monster II

Hallucination takes me—perhaps I dream awake
I'm taken from a burglary of Bliss
                              to the pit without A/C
Dissonance
            the flatted fifth
                      a clang so discordant
            chains and fetters rattle
like metal-legged locusts

The dark harmony reverberates
Shakes the Devil's crater
Till the walls meet the lava and the Sinning Sovereign
            calls that all his demons tune
                  to doom's true "Hallelujah"

Yet snickers for the visitor
            who strums a tonal opus
                  with his mission to enliven ink
                        until it's breathing just as he is

Currents and Tides Are Like Spacetime

After Larissa Szporluk's Isolato

Salmon migrate in twilight—
feathers floating past opals
flirting with the riverbed.
The stones are magic
gems. Charcoal briquettes
lit in Eden. Sent to boil broth
slowly. Sent to teach the school
to be a bird. Then to watch it
flap across a newly arid basin
hungry for what it was
unsated in the air
saturating the river with lies—alive
until the truth is washed away.

Wren Warbling

After Eryn Green's Eruv

A wren rests on a ledge outside Gus's bars
            It sings of cycling—
"The route for orchid bicycles is through the garden"

                              It flits away

What would it sing in a birdcage? Gus wonders

No Sabbath passages herein
In here—

            Heresy

View from a Zoo

After Maurice Manning's Lawrence Booth's Book of Visions

In the prison yard,
Gus climbs an imported Indian almond tree—
Ripe fruit. Tasty leaves. Comfy branches.
Nice view of the river.
He twists sticks (to replenish his cot)
and spies a horse, liquored
as a pirate's liver, charging madly down
the muddy bank all wobbly.
Its target—a retriever making fast tracks
of clovers toward a field
downriver. The plastered galloper
makes gains on the skedaddler
and Gus, a dog gorilla, wishes
he could punch the drunk ravager
in its big ugly nose. A young human grabs
for the reins—to yield
the horse and save the dog.
His skull caves under a cast iron shoe.
Gus looks on, frozen. The river rises
to wash the boy's wound
but it soon takes him. The dog gains a step.
But the submerged human
must have been its friend because it turns,
facing the wild bronco, fuming
slobbery fireballs and gnashing its teeth.
Mid-gallop—*Thud!* The horse drops dead.
Gus's uncle once told him about running drunk—
"Bad for the heart," he said.

One Flew Over the Zoo

Gus hacksaws one final bar with his owl talon—
the warden's horse won't catch him tonight

He rushes the yard...
                   the almond tree   and leaps

In the people city, Gus smells rot
He'd like directions to the garden
But he can't speak human
And he looks like shit

But we just met

After Richard Siken's Crush

Words taste like street-swept curb dirt, asphalt
                                    gravel and cigarette butts
        My teeth shatter into rice
                Jagged kernels cling to the sockets

Crunching compulsively
                                    Gums peel

Ripped to the jawbone

Two icebergs melt
        Words wave beneath a pool of dark red
                        cells in which I wade

rising past my shins

Submerged
                Quickly—by meeting the pool halfway

        Puréed lungs
                        prevent drowning—

I trade speech and air for life

The river leaves me my limbs
The moon plays Twister with my hands to teach me
                        sign language

before I'm washed away

Gusenstein's Monster III

Digging up I am unearthed
Seeds of science sprout around me
Insistent on their genius
    weeds of reason feed a crowd
        beleaguered laws embossing sand
          the tines of time erase
      before the penners
    make it to the punctuation

Lipped whistles splitting leaves
    the nearest instrument in weeds
        I pluck a blade
          to rouse my poem
            like a snake charmer

But piercing fails to sway
    my creature's rise   from print and page
        There are no walls
          inside the universe   for echoes

If you love something…

A poem is not forced
      It is cajoled—

Show a portrait of a monarch to a caterpillar
      But pretend the picture is a mirror
Cautious, the caterpillar sews a parachute and falls
      asleep testing its quilted cloud

After its metamorphosis
      show the butterfly a mirror
Though true to the portrait
      the young monarch churns at its reflection—
its spots are not as it likes

It jumps to flight and leaves
      the parachute for the poets

Part 2

Nuclear

po-e-try: n. 1 scar-farming flower plow. **2** Grace glasses.
3 Messiah of fireflies. **4** matchstick mushroom cloud. **5**
transcendentalist panhandler. **6** roundabout glue gun.

Day Break

Dawn is a mushroom cloud
across a lead horizon. People rise
like magnets. The sun paints
stars upon our skin—its brushwork
patterned in conversations with constellations.

Drawn to forests and farms but chicken
of shadows cast by raptors and scarecrows
we huddle into hovels and call them
"sanctuaries." Still comes the sun...

Air is flame

Earth is fusion charcoal

And we are matchsticks

So brave the wilderness and carve
a homestead. Tend the garden with your hair
on fire. When the rooster crows
inspect the coop—
an egg cracks when life begins
and when it ends.

Out of Many

A quarter is a crystal ball
spinning. I ask Washington
What do you see?
"Heads," he shouts
musket aimed. Heads it is.

Coin-pursed
I travel to a palm reader.
What do you see?
"Tails say the lines
but they waver," he rasps.
I dump my purse, and my quarters
land tails up on the table.

I search for shelter
penniless. An alley-beggar
lifts a tin mug and his quarters
rattle. "Take one, young Lazarus," he says.

I flip it high into lamped darkness.
"What do you see?" he asks.
A choice of fates, I confess.
He laughs. "You're more blind than me."

He snatches the quarter
as if a fly. "Here, run your fingers along
the trenches until you see a coin."
I feel the rigid lip of a disk.
"Exactly."

Emaciated

Dad calls me "emaciated"
over the smell of marinara.
I wonder what he means—
He likes thoroughbreds and he bets on maiden races.

So I ask him.
"I like thoroughbreds," I hear him say
as I lower my neck and whinny.
A bead of spaghetti sauce drips from his fork

onto his starched collar. I ask again.
"You look skinny," he clarifies.
I look at my plate—
Dad's found "The World's Best" chicken parmigiana

for six dollars. The sauce on his collar spreads.
But I am a funhouse mirror.
I look skinny? I muse.
I'll win a Derby. I'll wear its wreath   of roses.

Dirt

My toes clasp red clay
My heels auger

I uncover rocks, cornerstones—
big as buried pumpkins

Underneath, the soil is damp
It bends to the will of my feet

Weeds and briars stab me
Still, I dig roots

Glue Gun I

My horse, a shiny black stallion named Glue Gun, galloped into the home stretch six lengths ahead of the pack. The rest of the field was neck and neck—a thunderstorm chasing a clock. I clutched my first ever racetrack ticket and maneuvered through all the legs to get back to my father. I was grinning like I'd already won the lottery.

"Get up, Ten! Get up, Ten!" Dad yelled, clutching the steel railing.

The ten-horse's jockey whipped its hind legs in rhythm to my Dad's shouts. A buzz swelled from the infield to the grandstands. The ten-horse, Roundabout—a cream-coated palomino—narrowed its eyes, flapped its nostrils and broke away from the pack.

"C'mon, Ten! Get up!" Dad hammed. "That Ten went off sixty to one. And I've got him to Win!"

I stood up on the rail's bottom beam to watch.

Glue Gun's jockey whipped too, but the strikes only made my horse grimace and lag.

Meanwhile, Roundabout was a jet-engine dragster. He torched the racetrack and pulled even a half a furlong from the finish line.

"Get up, Ten! Get up!" Dad kept on.

The crowd revved like Paw Paw's table saw.

Grace

On a French Riviera beach lounger
    Mom skims *Harper's Bazaar*
wearing sunglasses in the shape of dragonfly wings
(a pair she saw Grace Kelly wear in *Elle*)

She blows a kiss to Prince Rainier
    (Dad) who waves back to her
from a frescoed portico in their palatial apartments
    before returning his attention to *The Beverly Hillbillies*

Mom takes off her sunglasses
    slips them
        into her handbag
           & transforms
                into Lisa Fremont
Her beach lounger flickers into a daybed
    inside a Greenwich Village apartment
Brandy and cigarettes
    replace the Mediterranean spray

Dad (L.B. Jefferies) sits across the room
    in a wheelchair   in a cast
        with his leg elevated
watching his neighbors
through the zoom lens of his camera

Finally, one concerned neighbor pays him a visit
& breaks his other leg at the end of the movie

The credits roll as
Dad slumps in his wheelchair
        snoozing
                in two-legged, thigh-high plaster PJs

while Mom lies on the daybed
        reaching for the glasses
                in her handbag

Dance

She raises her arms to pose—to brighten Dad's eyes
But fourth position wanes into a Little Teapot
     (Dad only smiles when he's free)
These slippers were too tight, she thinks
My leotard was ugly

She closes her lips
     to hide her childhood
              ivories
Her sweat splinters the barre
Mom buys a new tutu

Dad sits in the risers at a basketball game

So she practices
Masters each Arabesque
An auditorium limelights
     her adagio while Mom jams
              a gun into Dad's ribs
                       in the balcony

A luminaire bathes the crowd
     as she bows
              She watches Dad scowl
                       & worm in his seat

She bows again   for the roses

"I don't want to dance anymore," she tells him
As she lowers her arms—to brighten his eyes

Lightning Bug Lantern

A mason jar replaces my nightlight

Summer drips from the jar onto my dresser—
but too slowly for A/C
    in mid-June
            Dad said

Katydids compete with my ceiling fan
to soothe me, and I sweat
until I fall asleep

At dawn I slide out of bed
to inspect my insect pets—
who'd kept me safe through the night

Five red-headed sunflower seeds
crawl up the glass

The rest (about thirty) are raisons
Littered about the bottom of the jar
           like radiating squirrel poop

I cry
Then I pine—
my big sister helped me stab
    these air holes—this lid is a tined-mesh

Outside, I help the few survivors out of the jar
I go back inside
    Plug my nightlight in again

Then I wash and dry the mason jar
    & shelve it away in a cobwebbed
        cabinet above the stove, hoping

if Mom ever notices the shotgun scar
    she won't blame me

Glue Gun II

Once Roundabout gained a nose on him, Glue Gun pinned his ears, opened his gait and lowered his head. The other horses were well off the pace now, their thunderstorm muted by the crowd's roar for the frontrunners. The clamor stripped flakes of paint off the gigantic green metal tote board behind me. I read my ticket [$2 to show on #3], looked back at the board to make sure I'd told Dad the right horse, and then I smiled—Glue Gun had first, second or third in the bag.

"C'mon! Stay up, Ten! Stay up!" Dad yelled.

Not knowing much about payouts, I decided second would be just as good—I wanted my Dad to win, too. "Stay up, Ten! Stay up!" I began to yell, in unison. Roundabout's jockey whipped and whipped.

Glue Gun's nostrils flapped like pterodactyl wings. But his breathing was relaxed. Measured. He pulled even. Gliding. Reestablished a lead. He was about to win.

And then a crack, like a hickory tree had snapped, echoed off the tote board. I winced while the metal rang. Glue Gun's body careened into the dirt. His jockey launched from the saddle over the railing. Into the barbed hollies of the winner's circle.

Granite Pebbles

I gift Dad whiskey for ten Christmases before I
know why—
    granite is animate
        while a bottle drips
Whiskey rolls from his lips into a smile—
I am the architect-son of a stonemason

Granite turned my Dad into a statue
So I dig shallow graves into my skin—
    where the pebbles lie—
        & build an aquifer

I shovel and chisel
    Shovel and chisel
        till my blood is filtered
           through the rubble

I stitch up a ripped scar
    & etch another headstone: "Granite Pebbles"
drinking whiskey for ten Christmases before I know why

Glue Gun III

"What's that screen for?" I asked a minute later as two men rolled a six-foot square green tarp affixed to a metal frame onto the racetrack. Glue Gun was on his side, fifty feet from the finish line. His left front leg shook as he held it above the dirt. Roundabout and the other horses were nearing the stables at the other end of the track.

"They're going to have to euthanize it," Dad answered me.

"Euthanize?"

The two men set the screen in front of Glue Gun and walked over to a gate where an ambulance idled.

"A racehorse's legs are way too small for their bodies," Dad continued. "A break usually shatters the bone and won't ever heal right. Now c'mon. I'm going to have to cash my ticket at the IRS window!"

I hustled to follow him back across the infield, then down the steps into the tunnel under the racetrack—where I dropped my ticket into a sea of them.

Brown Honeysuckles

Drought

A mile and a sixteenth
     away from me
a honeysuckle vine meets a trellis

And I have two horse pies
baking in the sun's oven

My boot soles tote manure often—poorly
Extremities (edges) cook first
It assaults my steps like glued stones

Still I run
I am the "Brown Green Thumb Warrior"—
a fleet-footed fecal foliage physician
                    and I can fly

At last I arrive to paste moist chips with balled fists
into the intersection of Earth and Vine
Then I crumble
     dry chalky flecks
               beneath the trellis's
                    thin wooden posts

I stand and shower the ground with spit
I thrash and sing a rain dance

The sour reek decays   into perfume

Part 3

Allegory of the Shell

neu-ro-lin-guis-tic pro-gram-ming: n. 1 elephant drill.
2 turtle backflip. **3** gorilla whistle. **4** grizzly rooster crow. **5**
donkey blindfold. **6** tiger podiatry.

Man in the Moon

A runner's high slaps me as I reach my favorite segment of the trail—a serpentine quarter-mile that snakes the river. Orion's an inch above the horizon, his belt bright as stage lights. I look for the moon but find a clear night sky mottled with fireballs.

Must be new tonight. Too bad.
Wait…

As a boy, I used to stare at full moons. Squinting, eyelids teeming with ant legs, I blacked out everything but that glowing circle. Then I whispered, "the moon becomes all that I see. A part of me. It frees my soul. It is a hole," over and over. It cast a spell. The moon became a portal—an open doorway into a world of light hidden behind a black sheet. I felt warm when the moonbeam wrapped around me—a newborn swaddled in a nursery. Then I floated into the sky, rising up a lunar tractor beam like a bank deposit. It tickled, the moonlight, pouring between my toes and fingers—like wind applying lotion. It massaged my scalp and seduced my mind to goo. But for some reason I always opened my eyes before I made it to the moon, or beyond.

How could I have forgotten about that? So many years have passed.
I grew out of it? Lost the magic? Maybe the other side just stopped calling me?

Endorphins fade, and the serpentine settles
behind me. Orion is still up ahead, beaming.
I sprint, hoping to rekindle opiates, and I ask
the Hunter if I'm still allowed behind the sheet.
He points his sword at me, then (from his bow)
shoots an arrow at the slightest hint of a sliver of a
crescent, and I race him home.

Don't worry, the moon remains unharmed—
Orion's arrows fly on this side of the sheet.

Cinderella

Life is Disney.
Pixilate my atomic structure
in Technicolor bubbles.
Rhyme, my fairy godmother.
Bippity-bobbity-boo my genes
and pimp my pumpkin.
A handsome stranger awaits
my animation, stuck in
a cartoon castle. Dust up the forest.
Morph its critters
into horsepower. Let's get this
coach a-rollin', Wizard.
Glass slippers feel like cold bricks
swinging from butter knife blades.
It's rickety inside this hollowed husk,
and my feet hang
off the seat. (No cartoon
immunity for ornery
footwear.) I stare at fresh sorcery.
At feet of pinpricked glitter. And place
faith in magic wishes—faith these shoes
won't shatter or break
and stab me. Look for me at court.
I'll be dancing with the
debonair. Watch me bobble and bounce.
Will I bleed?

Turtle Training

I'm TJ the Turtle
I have an organic weather-stripped camper on my back
If it rains, I'm smiling dry inside
If I tire, it's night

It'd be easy to hunker down in my bunker
It is a bit of weight—
        an owl prescribes me eucalyptus inhalers
and my chiropractor is the hind leg of a hippopotamus

But I keep it moving
Maybe it's my hot rod paint job
Maybe it's because Aesop made me an athletic role model
Maybe it's the laps I jog and the chin-ups I do every day

Maybe it's the tiger

Due to our shells
turtles have unusual relationships in nature
For example—
A gorilla is my alter ego
A bear is my alarm clock
An elephant is my teacher
A butterfly is my navigator
And the tiger? Well—

The tiger's name is Colt
But call him "Sir"
or he'll take out your kneeCAPS

He likes to argue. Well… to shout
A loudmouth—an ALL CAPS guy
A volume debater

A bully—
a coward who picks fights
    and CAPS a punch with a tire iron or a crowbar

Thinks he's a mafia Don or a gangster
But he's a sycophant—
    wears khakis and logo polos
            with ball CAPS to cover a bald spot

Claims "hard work's all ya need to succeed"
    while freeloading
Hates ivory towers—
    wants CAPS and gowns replaced
            with "Real World Edge Occasions"

Colt got elected mayor a while ago
He gerrymandered the city limits into a headless octopus
    and built the public coffers into lab rat feeders
Damn Charter's got no CAPS on his term neither

But Colt's down by the river today
    trying to bullseye bottleCAPS
His aim's as bad as a boozed-up bat's
I'm hoping for a ricochet

Little known nature fact—bears sing
But it's just us turtles who hear the music

Since I was a hatchling
Mama Grizzly's yawns have sounded like a music box
    until I stick my head out of my shell—
The forest gave me and my sister a classical alarm clock
    and heavy metal warning siren all-in-one Bear
Thankfully, Mama G (that's what we call her)
        understands—
    she loves us even though we're just two turtles
(Poor Papa Donkey doesn't like the noise at all
    so he puts carrots in his ears)

One morning
    Mama G's cock-a-doodle-doo was ALL CAPS
I peeked through my shudders—
Mama G was upright, tall as a tree
    growling and biting the air
My sister CC's shell was closed

I hit the snooze bar

chopin   chopiN   chopIN   choPIN
    chOPIN   cHOPIN   CHOPIN
CHOPIN CHOPIN   CHOPIN   CHOPIN

It occurred to me gradually—
    Mama G was too loud
    Something was wrong

I opened my shell—

GRRRRRIRONMAIDENMEGADEATHSLAYERRR
    jagged brown fur curdled into sweat-soaked daggers
       Steam streamed from Mama G's snout
         and whipped the forest
           BLACKSABBATHGODSMACK

Following her line of sight

I saw HIM

creeping through thick blades of vegetation
    camouflaged by the strobe
       of sun-splayed rays
         against his stripes

HE leapt from the underbrush

CHOPIN CHOPIN CHOPIN CHOPIN CHOPIN

crash

When I came to
  the river growled next to me
  and the world was upside down

Little known nature fact—bear paws lack
the dexterity to flip a turtle shell
Mama G fumbled and muffed till it was clearly hopeless

She collapsed into the mud
and cried

"The tiger took her. The tiger took CC," she wept

I closed my shell
Pitch-black was upside down

* * * * *

Sorrow slaps bass guitars
two strings at a time
high up the neck
whammy bar
glides down the octaves
thumps a pulse
flicks a pickup switch
loops a blues beat

features a flute—

a misty forest reverie
whets the bassline

as treble clef dewdrops
splash cricket legs

* * * * *

Near a hemp-scented hop field
a pinwheel spins in the sunshine

It emits a storm-colored
strobe-lit vortex time machine—
a spiral straw in a juice box

So I take a sip

It sucks me

Prone as a log in a river
I float toward its propeller

Little known nature fact—
    bears and elephants are friends

That night I awoke to a pulse—
    polished riverbed stones
        pounded into pebbles—
louder than Mama G's MANOWAR

When I opened my shell
I saw a pewter elephant
    with big floppy ears
            lumber across the river
Mama G rose with a smile
    and hugged the percussive pachyderm
(Poor Papa Donkey's ear-carrots weren't big enough
    to mute elephant steps, so he hee-hawed upriver)

"Hello, TJ. I'm Ellie," said the elephant
    extending her trunk for me to shake
"I believe I can help you
First lesson—because it's the most important one—
    your shell's bow tie is a picture
            of your pathfinder butterfly"

"What!?!" I snapped
Mama G chuckled KORN

"That bow tie on the front of your shell
Directly below your head
The one that is ordinarily above your head
It's paired with your butterfly guide, TJ"
Ellie explained

Mama G had taught me about elephants
     eggheaded   long memories   rarely tiger food
But she hadn't mentioned their riddles

Can't you just flip me over with your trunk or something?
     I asked

* * * * *

Close your eyes, TJ

Let your shoulders erupt into warheads

Your skull   is a cannonball

Fangs rip through your gums

Your neck fans out like a cobra's

Your chest flexes into cinder blocks

Your abs are a brick wall

And your back is a pile driver

Now, picture CC
peering out her shell
            as the tiger paces

Open your eyes

Now, bite down on every plant
stem or stalk you see and strain
      your neck until they are uprooted
            or you are upright

* * * * *

Look at your reflection
    in the river, TJ

                          It's too choppy

The view takes some getting used to
But if it's too rough right now
    you can always try again later
Or maybe you'll find calmer waters
downriver

                But you can see my bow tie yourself
          Why can't you just tell me what it looks like?

It's a little known fact of nature—
animals learn best when they work
to discover things for themselves

                Then why do I need you here?

Now now
I am here to confirm when you've seen
your reflection and to redirect you
when you've been fooled
by distorted images
in the river

Hmm

It's a green butterfly, isn't it?

You've barely even tried, TJ

Red... with yellow speckles?

Get to work, you

Little known nature fact—
turtles get along with everyone
    Except—if a tiger pokes at a snapping turtle too long
       the snapping turtle will bite down on tiger toe
         so stubbornly the foiled predator will have to
            gnaw off its own digit just to free itself

Ellie knows everything about nature
She spent weeks teaching and training me

I'm a snapping turtle, and CC is a box turtle
Mama G's always called us "Night and Day"
Little known nature fact—
        the forest compliments who we are
         with who we aren't

I finish another chin-up   Release my bite

A newly familiar bow tie flutters above me
        and floats into the forest

An orange blur with flitting black ribbons
   meanders the breeze like a milkweed seed
     then stills upon the clumpy-haired rear
       end of Poor Papa Donkey (who is blindfolded,
         yoked to a fancy carriage in a field
           and sporting an even fatter pair of
             carrot earplugs)

My pathfinder (monarch)
       flicks from the senseless burro
               onto the coach door's golden handle

A pile of bones
     lies beneath the carriage—
             skulls sit atop an ivory bramble
                 My heart sinks

I sneak closer—   no shell

HE must have CC locked up inside, I surmise

I bite down on a bejeweled wheel spoke
     and pull myself up
Then I jump for the door and chomp-land on the handle

The plan was to do another chin-up
then jump inside the coach
But instead

the door flies open

and I swing out

like a streamer

Then just as quick

I come swinging back

lockjawed to the door

It slams shut into the latch

The momentum hurls me vertical

So I unchomp
and swing over the door

Right into the downy mane of my foe(!)

My arrival awakens HIM
(Tiger irises look a lot like orange daisies
    under celluloid film)
I close my eyes for a split millisecond—
    to let my shoulders erupt into warheads
            and all that—then scuttle down a paw

where I sink my psychosomatic fangs

HE starts thrashing and bucking around
    like I poked HIM with a branding iron
HIS claws gash the purple velvet
    upholstery until it's snowing white
            wisps of cotton
Then HE kicks the door off
    those oiled-up hinges
            and we avalanche onto the clearing
(All the while HE's screaming and hollering
        worse than Poor Papa Donkey did
            that time he got buried
                under his carrot trove)

Once HE regroups
    HE slams me against the bones
            Kicking
            Stomping   until the pile's gone
But my shell doesn't crack

HE smashes me against the metal
    luggage trunk   until I'm denting titanium

Still my shell doesn't crack

Then HE reverts to bucking and thrashing
So I clamp down harder—
>   *Tiger toe tastes of sweaty feet*
>   *But a tiger's blood is sweet*
>   *It's brown as muddy water*
>   *But it's syrup, and tangerine*

"YEEEOWWWWWRRRRRGGRRRR," HE emotes

Yee-Haw! I battle plan: Just got to hold on and I
might gnaw this thing clean off

I'm flinging and flopping
>   like a shutter in a hurricane
>   (but feeling like the hurricane)
>   when two small creatures part the forest

I almost release my bite when I see her

"No! Stop! Oh No! Please Stop! TJ! TJ!" CC yells
>   running toward the brawl
>   as fast as a box turtle can

CC's companion, a fuzzy brown marmoset, shrieks
>   then bolts back into the woods

"Oh No! Stop! TJ!" CC hollers again
    much closer already

I got this, Sis. It's going to be okay, I think
Surging with self-righteous firepower

                I crack HIS phalanx

Then, sudden flames—something bit me
    I look down at CC clamped like a vise

             onto my own back foot

      Staring back at me

with fireball-eyes

What the hell!?!   I let go
        CC and I fly across the field
           and coconut-smack
       into an almond tree
     at the edge of the break
Then we bounce back into the field
              belly up

Preferring a reprieve to HIS wrath
    HE limps over to the mangled carriage
The door falls off as HE climbs inside
(Poor Papa Donkey sleeps on)

CC lies upside-down and turtled up next to me
I am (of course) back on my feet in no time

I push CC over

You could have hurt HIM, TJ!

               Huh? CC, are you okay?
               Let's get out of here!

I'm not going anywhere!

               B-b-but HE'll be back!
               HE'll kidnap you again!

No, no, no, TJ
WE have an arrangement

               An arrangement!?
               Like for when HE'll eat you!?
                     CC, C'mon!

Just calm down
    and let me explain

                Explain fast, CC
                I can see your pathfinder
                butterfly right now and it's flying
                    next to mine
                        as they hightail it
                            into the forest

Sounds like you could do some explaining yourself
Anyway, here's what happened
    HE used to eat only fruit—
            fruit that grew right here in this clearing
    This used to be an orchard, TJ
    With apple trees, peach and pear trees
        even grape vines

                CC, this is a barren field!

Sure. Now it's a barren field

See, a year ago
    a herd of deer passed through here
    and devoured everything they could reach

                CC...

Just listen, TJ
        a few months after the deer left
        when HE was already weak from waiting
        for all HIS food to drop from branches
        a troop of monkeys came along and ate
        all the rest of the fruit
To make things worse
        all their swinging and binging
                in the canopy
                        killed all the trees
So you see, TJ
        HE has to eat them—
                to survive
                        until HE can regrow the trees

                                CC, we need to leave here
                        That's all just a bunch of horseshit

You don't know HIM, TJ!
COLT doesn't want to do it!
But when HE brings the orchard
        back, it will be worth it...
                for the monkeys too
                You'll see

                                CC, I love you
                                HE is a tiger!

HE needs ME, TJ!
That's why HE came for ME
     HE needs MY help

                              Help?
                    You were luring that monkey?

They really are stupid creatures
They almost destroyed the entire food chain

                    What has HE done to you!?!

HE keeps ME safe...
     unlike some other animals I know
Where is Mama G, by the way?

                         Little known nature fact—
                    fights between bears and tigers
                    are always draws—so snapping
                    turtles are nature's divine equalizers

Okaaaaayy...
C'mon, TJ
     Stay here—with US...
                    and Poor Papa DonKEY
I'm sure I can smooth things over with COLT
     eventually

I need for you to trust me, CC
We need to leave this place

I'm not going anywhere, TJ

Then neither am I.

Acknowledgments

Thanks to the editors of the *Vortex Magazine of Art and Literature,* Vol. 41, for publishing a version of "On a Soapbox."

Gratitude to Che Elias and Six Gallery Press for this publication.

Thanks to pfflyer at Morguefile.com for the cover photo which has been modified from its original version at https://morguefile.com/p/55877&/. And thanks to Morguefile for its forum.

Thanks to Robert Balentine, Chris Beaumont, Eric Binnie, Wendy Blackwood (my Penny Patterson), Taylor Brady, Audrey T. Carroll, Énbarr Coleman, Drew S. Cook, Shane Allen Curry, Mikayla Davis, Christian DeVries, Benjamin C. Roy Cory Garrett, Nicole Godfrey, Lea Graham, Coty Greenwood, Cassie Hayes, TJ Heffers, Rachel Hoge, Jake Honea, Tyrone Jaeger, Asha Jones, Kirk Jordan, Stacy Kidd, Joe Kramer, Mark Lager, Steve Lance, Liz Larson, Briget Laskowski, Scotty Lewis, Sandy Longhorn, Bob May, Alex McAnulty, Shua Miller, Devon Norris, Garry Craig Powell, Sarah Scarbrough, Callie Smith, Mark Spitzer, Heather Steadham, Jan Stone, Matt Stroman, Sabrina Sullivan, John Vanderslice, Stephanie Vanderslice, Beau Wilcox, the Arkansas Writers MFA Program and the University of Central Arkansas.

Above all, thank you, Mom.

Made in the USA
Middletown, DE
18 March 2020